the baby bomb

the baby bomb

GOVIND SANDHU

Illustrated by

ALLEN SHAW

HARPERCOLLINS CHILDREN'S BOOKS

First published in India by HarperCollins *Children's* Books 2026
An imprint of HarperCollins *Publishers*
HarperCollins *Publishers* India, Cyber City,
Building 10-A, Gurugram, Haryana-122002, India
www.harpercollins.co.in

2 4 6 8 10 9 7 5 3 1

P-ISBN: 978-93-6569-066-8
E-ISBN: 978-93-6569-721-6

Illustrated by Allen Shaw
Typeset in 12/20 Big Caslon by Aaryama Somayaji

Printed and bound at
Nutech Print Services Pvt. Ltd.

HarperCollins Publishers, Macken House, 39/40 Mayor Street Upper, Dublin 1, D01 C9W8, Ireland

*

CONTENTS

THE SCHOOL YEARS

He was born into a legendary family. His grandfather, after all, was the real deal—'Fat Man'—who had, in a single stroke, ended the Second World War. There were tall tales about how he had saved the world from destruction by being the first atom bomb in the history of mankind. People still talked about the day his grandfather was taken out and strapped onto a plane flying for hours over the Pacific Ocean in one of the most secret operations ever undertaken by a bomb. Fat Man was IT—no single bomb had ever created so much destruction. The stories about his legendary mushroom were folklore. Little Baby Bomb had always been intimidated by his family history and lineage.

Life at school was never easy; Baby always felt that he was different. He had a tender heart and a thoughtful little mind, often pondering about his own existence and its purpose. Baby was gentle and sensitive by nature, and while being in one of the best production and training facilities was a privilege, it was also a curse as you were surrounded by the best of the best at destruction. With everyone wanting to prove themselves, the environment was competitive, aggressive and challenging, preparing young bombs for the destructive mindset required to do the most damage they could and be proud of it.

This was quite different from who Baby was. Baby always questioned his existence, its purpose and introspected on the consequences of becoming who he was being trained to be. His lineage didn't make it easy either; it was taken for granted that he was a badass and Baby was pretending to be living the part. He even got himself a tattoo of a shark, for it provided him one more layer of pretense. Sharks represented the most fearsome and efficient killing machines in the oceans. His real self was quite contrary to the image Baby portrayed. In reality, Baby was afraid of heights and loud noises. He would often close his eyes while being taken up in a plane and would tremble inside with the loud noises that always surrounded him.

It was hard living this double life. Sometimes it got the better of him, like the one time in class when they were being shown videos of some of the bombs attacking and exploding. The teacher was explaining the different techniques of dropping in to get maximum impact and telling the young bombs how legendary they would be if they achieved such explosions. Baby innocently asked what if one does not want to explode, and there was pin drop silence in the class with everyone suddenly looking at him strangely. He immediately had to correct himself to say, 'I mean ... how does one ensure that they don't miss exploding ... be a shame if you didn't, right ... how do you make sure, sir, that no one misses exploding?'

The teacher explained, 'The mechanism is designed to explode on impact and there are enough trigger mechanisms inside to ensure it happens.' 'That's good to know, man,' said Baby in the gruffest voice he could make and looked around at the class trying to make sure he had not revealed his true self.

Other children would often sit around Baby wanting to hear stories about his grandfather, who would narrate them with passion and pretentious insensitivity. These experiences often left him emotionally exhausted.

Always making sure he never revealed his true self for the shame would be too much, not only as a bomb but for his whole family as well.

Baby would often confide in his diary which was the only time he could truly be who he was and share himself with those empty pages, which he knew wouldn't judge him. Popular and lonely at the same time, Baby's school life was a dream from the outside and a prison from the inside.

Finally, the day came when they would all graduate and be sent off to their respective ammunition dumps. There was a lot of excitement in the air about which location one would be sent to and what airplanes they would be working with. Everyone wanted to be close to the action; no one wanted to be in reserves sitting in storage. After all, the closer to the action you were, the faster the opportunity to prove yourself and make a name.

As expected, the best always made it to the dumps closest to the active warzones, if there were any. Baby got allotted to the most active zone and was cheered for it. He was torn inside, happy to be deployed so he could put an end to his misery but saddened that the culmination of his life would result in destruction!

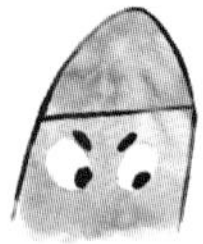

LIFE IN THE CLOSET

'Line up ... this is not drill, this is real life action, this is where you actually explode ... be the best you can be ... leave your MARK! Literally!!' These were the bellowing words of bomb leader 'Dead Pan'.

All the new bombs were scrambling to fall in line as they were introduced to the new ammunition dump in the base. This was going to be their new home, till they met with the explosive destiny that awaited them.

Baby was doing what he did best, pretending to be who he was not. The base was an action-packed zone. There were many interesting characters in the ammunition dump. Machine gun bullets, who were fast and always training to run; speed was all that mattered to these guys. There were rifle bullets who were focused on precision; they were always playing hide and seek and secretly hitting opponents with pinpoint accuracy. They were often meditating and finding focus—after all, being a sniper bullet was all about having patience and the right temperament. Then there were the grenades, they were very much like chubby Harley bikers—easy going, no precision required, 'just drop me anywhere and I will do some damage' was their attitude towards being deployed. It was no surprise that their tag line was 'I am handy, I am lazy and pack a punch'.

Other than the general ammunition quarters, in the base there was an exclusive area where there were some serious, large missile fellas. These guys were always talking about strategic targets and sophistication of use—this was an elite club. The missiles were slick and privileged, living in exclusive quarters and rarely disturbed. Their area was off limits to all the others with secure pass access being required to even enter. Finally, there was the category which gets strapped to planes and gets dropped—this was Baby's category. They were like paratroopers—they could glide down in groups and create a big kaboom working as a pack. All of them were well trained, disciplined and relied on teamwork. They were the first port of call for any assault. It always started with a rain of bombs before any of the others got engaged in battle. Team morale was very important to them to achieve their goals. 'One for all and all for one' was their approach to life.

The base was located quite close to the enemy lines. It was nestled inside a forested area with an airstrip just long enough for planes to take off. Since it was surrounded by forests, it could not be spotted or easily detected by the enemy. Inside the forest were underground bunkers which accommodated all the ammunition. Between the enemy lines and the base was an ocean front. It was one of the most beautiful places in the world, notwithstanding the military installments. Blue ocean front surrounded by green, largely undisturbed forests.

The base was full of different types of airplanes. There was constant activity on the airstrip with planes taking off and landing throughout the day. It was quite a wonderful experience taking flight from the hidden airstrip and coming out of the forest, low over the canopies of the trees before suddenly emerging onto the open ocean. It was beautiful but deadly.

There were two types of flights at the base, the first were the recon flights and then there were the loaded recon flights. Recon flights did not involve the bombs. These were the planes flying without any bombs to go and run reconnaissance on enemy territory. These were essentially low risk flights. Everyone knew they were entering enemy territory but never expected any engagement.

The loaded recon flights were different. These were training exercises for the planes and the bombs. The training flights were the ones where the bombs were loaded onto the planes, but the flight was not meant for bombing. Training flights were really designed for fortifying the nerves of those who had not seen battle before. It made it real for them.

Baby had been on a few of those. Loaded recon flights let the bombs get familiar with the planes and the environment for when the real deal happens. Thankfully for Baby, the few times he had been taken up, it had mostly been on night flights. It might sound counterintuitive, but Baby was happier going up at night, as he often kept his eyes closed throughout the flight due to his fear of heights. This way he could keep his secret, as no one could see him scared. He had a good sense of the terrain now.

He recognized a set of ruins which marked the enemy territory. The ruins always told him exactly where he was.

It was midnight and the bombs were being loaded onto the planes. Baby was getting ready for another loaded recon. They were briefed that it was going to be a dangerous recon deep into enemy territory. This meant that there was a small possibility of engagement with the enemy.

The loaded recon was being run by two planes called 'Dead Meat' and 'Jammed'. Dead Meat was known to be a fierce plane that never backed down from any call to action. He was also well known for his daring missions deep into enemy territory. As one of the most experienced planes on the base, it was expected that he would be the one flying the most dangerous missions.

There was a slight breeze blowing and an overcast sky. In the dark of the night, Baby was loaded onto Dead Meat. The full moon was lighting up the airstrip one moment and then hiding behind the black clouds making it pitch dark the next moment. As they headed down the taxiway, Baby was keenly aware of what it meant to be loaded onto Dead Meat. For many, it would be a privilege, but Baby was nervous, thinking of what a strange night it was. His stomach was churning, and he had an eerie feeling about it all.

The two planes took off. Dead Meat and his wingman, Jammed, headed into the dark skies. Baby had never ridden with Dead Meat before but expected it to be the same as the loaded recon missions he had done before. As they took off, the moon once again came out from behind the skies and Baby could recognize some of the landscape below. He could see them heading towards the enemy territory, flying low over the shining sea full of reflected moonlight. The breeze was getting stronger, and the clouds were getting thicker with every passing mile. Baby was trying to figure out where they were when the moon made one more appearance, and he saw the familiar ruins. In a blur they had crossed over into enemy territory.

Baby knew that anything could happen at that moment. He was hoping that it would be an uneventful night, but his heart was pounding, and his mind was racing in all directions. He was lost in his thoughts when suddenly flashes from the ground startled him.

'They are firing at us,' confirmed Jammed.

'Let's go silence those guns!' snarled Dead Meat as he swooped down into a dive with Jammed following in close.

The wind was blowing in Baby's face, mixed with a slight drizzle. The lights from Dead Meat's wings were flashing past him as gunfire lit up the sky. All the bombs on the wings were screaming war cries and preparing themselves for action. Suddenly, red lights started flashing, and one by one the bombs got released, screaming on their way down. Baby was scared and filled with panic.

Finally, the worst he had expected happened; his front clasp opened to release him. But Baby held on to it. The back clasp was also open, but while the front clasp tried to open again and again, Baby desperately held onto it by pushing into the screw. Dead Meat screamed, 'Go, Baby, go! I can't hold this dive much longer,' and just then the plane started pulling out of his dive.

It was too late to drop Baby. Dead Meat gave a look of contempt to the young bomb from the corner of his eye and started heading back to base. The ordeal was over. Baby was trembling as he held onto his clasp. Raindrops hit his face and mixed with the tears streaming down his cheeks in the wind. As terrifying as it was, Baby was even more terrified of what possibly awaited him.

What if Dead Meat saw it all, what if he exposed Baby ... what if ... There was complete silence throughout the flight back. The hollow feeling of emptiness and the fear of what would happen was unbearable. It felt like the longest flight Baby had ever been on and he hoped it never ended.

Baby heard the sound of the landing gear and wished he had let go as what awaited him might be worse than death. Jammed and Dead Meat touched down and taxied towards the hangars.

Dead Meat looked at Baby with disgust as he scolded him, 'What the hell is wrong with you! You could have used the wind to let go but you didn't ... I saw that'.

Baby had been trying not to make eye contact with Dead Meat but it was impossible to ignore his accusation. Baby knew Dead Meat's reputation and did not want to engage him in a dialogue which would only make matters worse.

Baby put on a brave face and just looked at the clasp, pretending like it wasn't his fault. It took all the courage in the world for him to find his voice. He looked at the clasp in frustration and yelled, 'Damn clasp!' he said, looking at Jammed to make sure he was heard. Just then, it occurred to Baby that Jammed had been behind him all this while and could have seen everything much clearer than Dead Meat. It was an awkward moment but just then, to his relief, the team arrived to dismount him from the plane and took him away.

Baby was put away to undergo repairs in his dropping mechanism. The word was out that Baby had refused to let go ... there were a lot of hushed up conversations taking place at the base about what had happened.

Some had already pronounced him guilty, while others were still wondering if it really was a mechanical fault. They refused to believe that Fat Man's lineage could be like this. A few days passed. Baby had been through a detailed examination process in isolation. It had worked out well for him as it kept him away from all the questions and allowed the rumours to rest. Baby was now ready for testing to ensure he was functional.

It had been a week since the episode. Baby was wheeled into the hangar and saw Jammed standing there. They both looked at each other and Baby smiled sheepishly at Jammed. Jammed smiled right back in a nonchalant way as Baby was strapped onto him. He tried to put on a brave face and got ready for testing.

He looked at Jammed with some enthusiasm and asked, 'Ready to test me?'

Jammed looked at Baby and replied, 'I will do it but, it's not my favourite thing to do'.

Baby was not sure what that meant. Did it mean that Jammed was like him, someone who didn't like destruction or did it mean that Jammed didn't like to drop bombs that don't do what bombs are supposed to do?

Baby's guilt was making him overthink everything anyone was saying to him. He was constantly trying to evaluate whether he had been exposed or was being judged.

As he was preoccupied in trying to make sense of the conversation, he found himself being released and with a thud, he fell onto the net below.

The testing process went on for a few days. Consequently, Jammed and Baby ended up spending a lot of time together.

Baby asked Jammed how he got his name. Jammed rolled his eyes and explained, 'Well, because I jammed'.

Baby looked confused, 'What do you mean 'You Jammed'?'

'That's exactly what I mean, I jammed', shrugged Jammed. 'On my first tour, I was so overcome with fear that my propellor jammed and I couldn't get going. Since then, I have been called Jammed,' he explained with a smile.

'I am sorry to hear that, it must be hard. How does it feel?', asked Baby.

'You have to live with the consequences of your actions. But it's time bound and stops bothering you after a while. This war action is not my thing really, I'd rather be a transport plane doing some service,' Jammed replied.

Baby could relate to Jammed and felt like he could open up to him.

'I know how you feel,' he said. 'This war thing is not my favourite either.'

Jammed nodded slowly, having known Baby's secret for some time. 'Must be hard being a bomb, killing all those people,' he asked.

'Yes, it is. And you're not doing anything to help by taking me up there,' Baby said as they had a small chuckle about it.

It was the last day of testing. As the sun set, the two new friends said their goodbyes and Baby was carried out of the hangar. It was the first time that Baby found someone to talk to about his hopes and fears. His heart felt lighter, and he was smiling after a long time.

THE GREAT ESCAPE

It was a bright morning when the silence was shattered by wailing of sirens. Everyone was woken up to a sense of urgency and chaos. There were voices on the loudspeakers—an offensive attack had been declared.

Armoured vehicles were starting to line up in a column and men were getting ready for battle. The base felt like a hub of frenzied activity. All the different kinds of ammunition were being prepared to be deployed. Soldiers were grabbing boxes of grenades and packing them into their kits, machine guns were being loaded and tanks were being prepared for a skirmish.

Baby and his group were being rolled out as the planes were supposed to clear the area before it was the turn of the ground forces. Everyone was cheering on Baby and his crew, 'Come on, guys, make it count! We are right behind you,' yelled the machine guns.

Baby was being taken towards the hangars and the first hangar had Dead Meat standing in it. Baby's trailer was turned towards Dead Meat and his heart skipped a beat. Just the thought of being strapped onto Dead Meat was petrifying. Dead Meat was looking straight at Baby with a menacing smile.

Just then someone shouted from the back, 'Pull it along!' and Baby's trailer made one more turn and got pulled into the next hangar where Jammed was standing. Baby and Jammed exchanged looks, it was a melancholic look that had a sense of finality to it. They both knew where this was headed. This wasn't a situation where he might have to drop Baby; it was a goal to drop Baby to his death. It was the end of the road of a brief but true friendship, with secrets that they would take to their graves.

Baby's destiny was clear, but who knew where Jammed would end up—

transporting something or torn by bullets in a blue sky. Jammed had a heavy heart knowing what was at hand, killing Baby was the job he had to do. Why? He could neither understand nor question the decision.

The weather felt as harsh as the violence that awaited them as Jammed taxied towards the runway. The morale all around was high and boisterous.

Baby had resigned to his destiny. He put on one last show as he screamed, 'Yeah, let's do it!' Baby's war cry resonated with others joining in with their own screams of bravado.

Jammed looked at him from the corner of his eye; he knew exactly what was going on in Baby's head. He was among the few who could see through the act.

Jammed and Baby exchanged one last look as Jammed's propellors sped up and started pushing him ahead onto the runway. There was no turning back now.

They were flying low over the sea to avoid being detected by radar. There was a lot of gusto around him, but Baby felt lost as he looked at the ocean below. He looked ahead to see Dead Meat starting to pull up. His heart sped up as he knew it was time for Jammed to follow his lead.

As they started to pull up, Jammed looked towards his wing to see Baby closing his eyes. He knew that Baby was scared of heights. Just then, he started flashing his red light as turbulence set in. Everyone was confused because they were not yet at the altitude to release bombs. This was not what was supposed to happen.

The pilots kept repeating the word 'Malfunction' in frustration and cursing Jammed, 'Goddamn ... Jammed ... You're one piece of junk!'

There was confusion and chaos inside the cockpit, as the pilots tried to figure out what was going on. The bombs were also wondering if they had been hit or something else had happened.

Then all of a sudden, Baby felt the clasp loosen and him getting released. He looked up at Jammed in confusion and fear. It was as if everything was happening in slow motion.

Baby saw Jammed pull up and felt himself floating in the air, flying solo. He looked up in a state of confusion and saw Jammed smiling at him. He heard his last words, 'Stay safe, little one!'

As he heard those words, there was a splash and down went Baby Bomb into the ocean. He had survived the fall but was now sinking. Everything was a blur. Waves of emotions flowed through him, emotions of shock, confusion and disbelief. As he sank into the water, he was amazed at his surroundings. The ocean was quiet and calm in contrast to where Baby had come from. He gradually lost consciousness as everything became hazy blue, and Baby resigned himself to his fate.

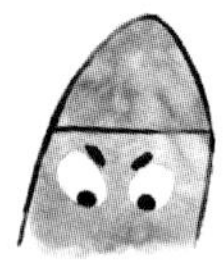

LIFE
IN THE OCEAN

Baby landed on the soft sand of the ocean floor with a gentle thump. After rolling around unconscious, he was woken up by a little shove. As he slowly opened his eyes, Baby saw a little shark nudging him. It was trying to push him over to see the drawing of a shark painted on his side.

'Hi, I am Ista,' the little shark introduced herself, beaming.

She pointed at the shark drawn on Baby and asked why he had that.

'You see, that's me,' she smiled.

Baby was still in a daze. It felt like a dream. He looked at his side where the drawing was and was amazed to see a shark in real life.

He wondered aloud, 'You are so friendly—' but she cut him off, '—Why, were you expecting something different?'

Baby's mind wandered off, remembering all the aggressive shark stories he was told just before one was painted on his side. He was about to say yes, but upon realizing his surroundings, quickly corrected himself, 'No ... no ... no ... of course not, you are nice ... that's why I have this painted here ...'

They were both curious about each other and curiously alone like each other. Ista and Baby soon became friends. She asked him how he ended up in the ocean. Baby made up a quick lie, explaining that he ran away from home as he was curious about the ocean. Ista was inquisitive and asked him what creature he was as she had never seen one like him before. Baby explained that he was a toy.

'What's a toy?' she asked.

He was surprised, but explained, 'It's something little children play with.'

They were excitedly sharing stories when Ista heard a voice in the distance and said her mom was calling her, so she had to leave.

Baby saw Ista swim away into the blue ocean. He wondered if he would ever see the only friend he had ever made again. Ista's presence had taken away the stark sense of loneliness in the vast ocean. As she faded away into the distance, the magnitude of it all finally started to sink in. Baby was in this unknown world, all alone. Before a sense of despair set in, Baby quickly reminded himself that it was still better than the world where he felt lonely despite being surrounded by others.

Still trying to make sense of it all, Baby rested against a rock when, to his surprise, he saw another bomb in the distance. He couldn't believe it. He squinted to get a better look through the water as he tried to see clearly. But before he could do so, a colourful school of fish approached and surrounded him as they swam past. Baby tried to look through them, but by the time they cleared, the bomb he thought he saw in the distance had disappeared.

Baby was confused whether he had actually seen it or if it was just his tired imagination. He turned back towards the rock he was resting on and noticed a pair of eyes looking at him from behind it. It was a creature he had seen before. Baby had seen an octopus before, painted on a plane, but this was the first live one he was seeing. Baby smiled nervously. In his mind, being painted on an airplane can only mean that the animal was dangerous. The octopus looked back and then vanished in a cloud of ink.

Baby had had a long day in this new environment. There was a lot to take in. Lodged against a small rock on the ocean floor and exhausted, Baby fell asleep, lost in his thoughts.

The next day, Baby had a pleasant surprise. Ista came back to visit him. Even though they had just met, there was a sense of comfort in seeing her. After all, she was his only friend in this new world.

Baby shared his experience about seeing the octopus. Ista laughed and explained that it was Octo. 'He is a sweet fellow, and one of the smartest guys around here,' she said. 'He's a little shy, but once you get to know him, he is quite cool really. But like I said, he is definitely the smartest guy on the ocean floor. He can do some pretty amazing things with those eight arms of his. Where did you see him?' she enquired.

Baby pointed to the rock. Ista dashed for the rock, and sure enough, Octo was behind it. Pulling him out, she introduced the two—Baby as the coolest toy kids could have and Octo as Mr Smarts.

Over a period of time, the three became good friends. Ista and Octo showed Baby around the reef. Soon, exploring the reef together became their favourite activity. They also played hide and seek a lot, and no points for guessing who won that game every single time.

Ista often asked Baby about his family. Baby was building his false life as he went along. He talked about toys and how they had such a satisfying life since they always made people happy. He would often spin his propellor to show them how he could swim. Baby had created this fantasy world for himself and his friends, of a life he wished he had but never did.

One day, Baby met Ista's mother and that's when he realized how big and lethal sharks could be. However, he saw their gentleness and how misunderstood they were by humans. They never want to hurt anyone and only hunt to satisfy their hunger.

One day, the three musketeers—as Ista, baby and Octo liked to call themselves—decided to go for an adventure to the edge of the reef, which was a forbidden place. There was a sharp edge at the end of a cliff, and it was famously known as the eel cliff.

They were there to see if they could spot an anglerfish, which shone in the dark. They had been warned about the eels and their colony down there. Eels don't like strangers, and definitely don't like them in their part of the ocean. Yet it was hard to resist the lure of seeing the mystical anglerfish with the bright light on its head.

The three musketeers started swimming in the easterly direction towards the cliff. Behind them, the reef started fading away into the distance. They could see the downhill slope of the cliff approaching. They pressed on, going down the slope, which was gradual but led to darker waters. They could also feel stronger currents around them as they looked at each other for support. Without realizing it, they started drifting faster than they thought and before they knew it, they were at the edge of the cliff.

The three were leaning over the edge when a sudden gust of current from behind pushed Baby off the edge. Octo stretched out and tried to grab Baby, but underestimated how heavy Baby really was.

Octo struggled to hold on, as Ista dived behind him and swam towards Baby to help him up from the other side. But before she could reach him, Baby slipped out of Octo's grasp and started sinking into the abyss.

Baby was in free fall. The water around him got darker with every passing second as he sank towards the bottom of the ocean. Ista felt scared and was not sure if she should chase him into the deep. Slowly, Baby disappeared into the darkness as Ista decided to pursue him into the dark waters. As she nervously went deeper, from the depths emerged a large shark carrying Baby up. Ista was relieved but scared, as the rescuing shark was none other than her mother, who had always warned them from going near the edge.

Ista's mother saved Baby's life and brought all of them to safety. Not wanting to embarrass her daughter in front of her friends, she didn't say much. But Ista looked sheepish and understood exactly why her mother had warned them.

This was among the many adventures the three of them had together. Baby had settled well into his new life with his new friends. Time flew by with the excitement of exploring this new world. His past life was but a memory which still haunted him sometimes in his dreams, but those dreams were fading away with the arrival of happier memories.

BEING FOUND OUT

It was a regular day in the ocean with everyone going about their business. The three musketeers were also making their plans for the day. From the depths, one could usually see the wake of a large ship as it sailed past. This happened so often that no one paid much attention to it. But unlike any other vessel passing by, this one was followed by a strange sound which no one had ever heard before. It was like a rumbling scream that pierced the air.

Everyone wondered what it was, but only Baby could recognize the sound of a plane diving through the air with its engines blaring. The sound immediately took him back to an array of memories; memories of a life he had almost forgotten. He was relieved to be deep in the ocean away from it all, and thanked god for the fact that it was all behind him and couldn't touch him now.

To his relief, the ship was fast disappearing into the distance, and the sound of the plane followed it. Everyone sensed it moving away from them and no one was more relieved about it than Baby. While he pretended that he didn't understand it, deep inside there was a sense of panic and relief as the sound decreased in intensity.

The relief had barely set in, when the fading sounds were shattered by a blast of current which surged through the water. The loud sound of an explosion surrounded everything. It was something that had never been experienced by anyone in the reef. The flash of light in the distance was hard to miss and the resulting shockwave shook everyone and everything.

All sorts of creatures were trying to hold onto something to avoid being blown away by the blast of current. As it passed, the ocean returned to its state of calm and you could see floating debris and oddly shaped objects in the distance. Slowly, some of the senior residents approached the area of the blast. It was always the sharks that led the way as they could smell anything from miles away and were the fastest. Seeing them make their way, Ista dashed towards them. She was looking for her mother in this confusion but was told to stay back ...

They could smell blood and there were streaks of red starting to appear in the water. Even before they could get closer, they saw one of their own floating towards them lifelessly.

It was Ista's mother. She had been too close to the explosion, and it had taken its toll. Her body was being prodded along by another shark, who was seriously injured and barely conscious himself. The other sharks quickly surrounded them and brought them both towards the reef where they lay Ista's mother to rest. Baby was petrified by what had transpired. He was hoping against hope that no one would associate the events of the day with him by identifying him or his kind as the cause of this destruction.

Thankfully, no such thing happened.

Days and weeks passed. Everyone was still trying to understand what had really happened that day. Ista was beside herself in grief and was trying to come to terms with the loss of her mother. She found solace in her two friends, Baby and Octo. Both had become her bedrock since her mother passed away.

The ocean was going through a change of seasons. This was when the currents changed in temperature and direction. It was an exciting time of the year as it meant the arrival of travelling guests, riding these currents while passing through; it was a time to catch up with old friends who travelled through the year. Ista was explaining the seasons to Baby, who was listening intently and found it all quite curious and exciting. She told him that it was the season for the turtles to visit. Baby had never seen a turtle and was quite curious to see them.

The turtles are quite exquisite with their hundred-year-old shells. The younger ones carry energy and smiles, while the older ones carry wisdom with them. Some of them stop at the reef to feed.

Scar was an old turtle who had been stopping at the reef for many years.

He was among the most well-travelled and oldest turtles; he was called Scar due to the scars on his shell. The old turtle was feeding on his favourite seaweed in the middle of the busy reef when he saw Baby. The expression on his face turned to one of panic. He immediately withdrew into his shell and tried to swim away, shouting for everyone to take cover and hide.

There was confusion all around him and Baby was left standing alone in the middle of the reef as everyone hid behind something or the other. There was an awkward silence with Baby in the centre of everything, standing all alone.

Slowly, all the creatures started to peek from behind their hiding spots. Scar resumed shouting again with fear in his voice, 'HIDE! HE IS GOING TO EXPLODE!'

'I have seen his type before ... that's exactly what happened some days back in this area too, right? You see these scars, these are from an explosion from one of his own kind!' explained Scar, pointing at Baby.

Everyone was confused as they stuck to their hiding spots. Baby had been with them for months and he hadn't exploded.

Ista heard all the commotion and made her way to Baby. She stood by his side, 'He is not some thing that explodes, he is a toy. Tell them, Baby,' she claimed emphatically.

Baby stood in silence and slowly looked up at Ista. She looked at him in disbelief, stammering, 'I don't understand.' Baby's eyes misted over, and he looked down in shame.

Scar rushed towards Ista and pulled her away from Baby. She swam away in disbelief and despair as everyone watched.

Baby had desperation in his voice, 'Yes, I am a bomb. I am sorry, Ista, I am a bomb, I was born a bomb but that is not who I am. I didn't choose to be a bomb. I am trapped in being a bomb. I don't want to kill anyone; I don't want to explode and hurt others. That's the reason I ran away—to find a new life. But I have put all of you at risk and I take responsibility for that. I have betrayed your trust. I thank you for the little time I got in your home.'

Baby looked at Ista for one final time. Ista had tears flowing down her cheeks as she and the rest of the reef's residents swam away into the darkness of the sea. There was silence all around. Baby's world had been shattered by the echoes of his past.

Baby had resigned himself to his circumstances and was ready to accept whatever fate had to offer him. His will to escape his destiny dissolved into the abyss of sadness that was his life.

The eels had always been suspicious of Baby. They rallied everyone to send him into exile to the wreckage of the ship which had killed Ista's mother on the far side, away from the reef. There he would not be a danger to anyone.

Baby was sad and alone near the wreckage. He spent his days reflecting on his life. The eels swam by on a regular basis to ensure that Baby was restricted to his new quarters.

A few weeks later, Baby saw Ista appear out of the darkness. Ista had had a chance to reflect on Baby's life and his dilemma.

Baby asked her to leave. He didn't want to put her at risk, 'I am very sorry, Ista, I genuinely never thought I was of any risk to you, but I am not so sure anymore. I am dangerous to be around and don't want to hurt you in any way, even by mistake. Please go away.'

But Ista refused. She wanted to hear the truth about Baby. She needed to understand why her friend had lied to her. Ista felt that knowing the truth would help her understand and reconcile with the loss of her mother.

Baby owed it to her to tell her the truth. For the first time, Baby told Ista about his real life. He told her about his family, the training, the mission, the desperation of living a false life and the eventual escape from it.

'What is it like to be a bomb?' asked Ista.

Baby replied, 'How do you think it feels when your whole life's purpose is to destroy all things made by God and you don't even have a choice in the matter?'

She could feel his sadness, as well as the desperation and tragedy of it all.

Baby explained how all bombs were brainwashed into making killing their goal in life and how being martyred was portrayed to be such a great thing. He could never understand it and so, he never fit in.

Baby expressed his deep desperation and exasperation with life, 'I wish I could get rid of this threat from my life and find a way to not explode.'

Ista innocently asked, 'Why not, have you ever tried to figure it out, there must be a way to disarm you.'

'I don't know.' Baby was unsure. 'I have heard of some legends of people who tried it and died trying. To be honest, I don't mind dying trying. If I fail, at least, it will end this miserable life, and if I succeed, maybe I can make a difference for others like me.'

In the meantime, the eels had been working hard through their network to try and find any other bombs in the ocean neighborhood and confine them to the wreckage.

One morning, Baby woke up to a noise in the wreck, only to find a thin, long bomb landing through the water from above. As he looked outside the wreckage, he saw a few turtles fading away into the distance. The eels had created a SWAT team consisting of sharks who could sniff out the bombs from a mile away, and hard-shelled turtles who could transport them, as they were well-protected by their shells in case of a mishap.

The long bomb looked very scared, just like Baby was when he had been discovered. 'Long' looked at the side of the ship as he descended into the water. He could read the half-scrubbed name on the hull—'Utah'.

Long's mind went back to his memories of sinking—he had looked up to see his colleague crash into Utah and explode. He also remembered seeing a shark getting caught in the explosion. He could see the shadow of a shark-shaped figure in the light of the explosion. He was still lost in his thoughts when Baby called out to him.

Baby nervously introduced himself. He told Long not to worry; he was in a safe place. Long appeared rather shy, but seeing as he was with another bomb, he, nevertheless, shared his story. He explained that he was a torpedo and was on his way to hit a ship when he got caught in a fishing net and his propellor stopped.

He exclaimed, 'That was it! For some reason I didn't explode and slowly sank to the ocean floor.'

Showing his scars, he explained how some sharks had tried to chew on him before the SWAT team arrived.

Baby said the ocean had changed him. Seeing the peace and tranquility around him, he had started to reflect on his life and realized he was better off living in hiding here than ever trying to explode. The two young bombs chatted late into the night and then finally fell asleep on the couch in the captain's cabin.

Next morning, Long woke up startled and panicked when he saw Ista swimming towards him. He called out to Baby, fearing the worst. He didn't have pleasant memories of sharks.

'Don't worry,' Baby tried to assure Long, 'That's Ista, a friend of mine.'

'You are friends with a shark!?' Long was shocked. Clearly his experiences had been different from Baby's.

Baby introduced Ista to Long, who was curious about his scars. Long explained how he and his colleague were fired at a ship and while his friend exploded, he failed to do so. Baby explained that Ista lost her mother in that explosion. Long felt very embarrassed, 'I am sorry, I really am. I don't do that anymore. I have taken a vow to not explode.'

Soon enough, Ista started bringing Octo to the wreckage to meet Baby and Long . The four of them became the best of friends and secretly hung out in the wreckage of Utah. A sense of normalcy started to return to their lives. It was a hidden life, but it was comforting to have friends who didn't judge you.

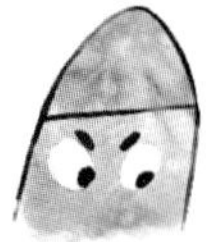

THE LONG STORY

But besides playing together, Octo, Baby, Ista and Long were pondering on something serious. They became a team determined to solve the challenge of defusing a bomb. And they started it all by discussing why Long did not explode.

What was different in his environment that stopped Long from exploding? Clearly, the only thing that happened which was out of the ordinary was that Long had got stuck in a fishing net.

Long was trying hard to remember the fateful day. His mind flashed back to that moment. He remembered being dropped from a plane that was flying really low and then plunging into the water ... he remembered his friend screaming past him as he felt something hit him in the face. But he easily tore through it and sped on, only to feel hamstrung at the back. Long vividly remembered the net getting entangled in his propeller. The net tied up into knots, jamming his movement and no matter how hard he pushed, it locked him up and stopped him in his tracks.

The last thing Long remembered was losing that struggle against the net and feeling lightheaded as he started to slowly sink into the dark waters, only to see a huge flash of light as he took a final glance to watch the shadow of a shark.

The next time Long regained consciousness, it was with a sharp sensation of pain as he found himself being attacked by sharks, their teeth scraping against his metal skin ... after which he passed out again.

Ista stared out into the light blue ocean above, filled with grief. Baby reached out and held her fin as Long looked down at the floor in shame, unable to look her in the eye. 'I am fine,' she said as she wiped off the tears.

'We should make sure no one ever has to suffer the fate Maa did.'

Octo hugged her with all his eight arms. He pointed at Long's tail, 'Do you mind if I take a closer look?'

Long replied, 'Not at all, that is why I am here.'

Octo felt that the tail not spinning was the only exception to the circumstances. He wanted to open Long and take a look inside. But opening a bomb was fraught with danger and they decided that it was best to call two of their turtle friends to shield them in case something went wrong. So, they had to postpone the idea for a day. They didn't want to put pressure on Long either. They all decided to take the night off and meet the next day. It was decided that Ista would talk to the young turtles for their help.

It was a long night for everyone. For Long, it was so because he didn't know what to expect, and for Baby because his fate could very well be tied to Long's.

LEARNING TO DEFUSE

It was a nice calm day in the ocean, but the mood near the wreckage was anything but that. The anxiety was clearly visible on everyone's face. There was a sense of nervous excitement as they slipped their way into the wreckage, looking over their shoulders to ensure no one had seen them.

Ista and the turtles had come to the wreckage. They all assembled in the engine room which was deep inside the hull of the ship. If something were to go wrong, they wanted to make sure no one outside was affected by it.

Octo looked at Long and asked, 'Are you ready, buddy?'

Long joked, 'I have been ready since I was born.' You could see he was trying to turn it into a lighter moment to take the pressure off the others.

Long lay down on the makeshift table, 'Alright, guys, let's do this.'

He looked at the turtles who approached him and surrounded him with their shells. Long was lying face down as Octo cautiously began unscrewing the nuts on his back.

The turtles were crouching with their shells facing Long, with Octo carefully working from behind them, opening one screw at a time. He gently put the parts onto the side as he opened Long's metal cover. It was the 'aha!' moment everyone was nervously waiting for.

'So far, so good,' said Ista, trying to hide her worry.

'Yeah. Not being dead is a good start,' added Baby, whose nerves weren't settling anytime soon.

Long was looking over his shoulder to try and see what was going on when Baby told him to stay still. Octo slowly slid the cover to one side to reveal his insides. Everyone, including the turtles, was in awe of what lay beneath the metal cover. No one had ever looked inside a bomb before. Baby himself was full of curiosity and fear.

Everything was still and tense. Suddenly, a current passed through the water and triggered the propellor in Long's tail, and just like that the mechanics of the bomb revealed itself.

Octo gazed at the sight in wonder and noticed a long screw turning every time the propellor rotated. The turning screw pushed inwards, gently putting pressure on a point inside Long's body.

Octo could see a spring linked to the screw and the pressure tip. He carefully beckoned Ista and asked her to hold the propellor and stop it from turning anymore. It seemed like with a certain amount of movement of the propellor, the pin got pressed to activate the bomb. 'That's enough for today,' Octo sighed in relief as everything had gone without incident and he started putting Long back together.

It had been a nerve-racking few hours. Everyone was relieved that nothing went terribly wrong and nobody was hurt. They spent the rest of the day discussing the findings and what Octo had seen. Long was the most curious, since he was the only one who had been unable to peek inside his own body.

Octo drew what he had seen to explain to Long the jumble of wires, screws and springs inside of him. They were trying to relate what they saw with how Long felt when the screw was turning. There was a lot of discussion, after which they finally concurred that this was the mechanism which triggered the bombs.

Baby started introspecting, recounting all those times when he had sped away with his friends pushing and pulling him, never knowing that he could have easily exploded. He felt horrible about how careless he had been by putting his friends in mortal danger. He was now more determined than ever to defuse, and find a way to defuse and free others like him.

The four decided to start testing ways to check their hypothesis. Baby insisted on being the one to do any further testing and not put Long, who had already done more than enough, at risk.

It was another sleepless night in the wreckage as everyone prepared for the next day, when Baby would be tested. They decided to sleep together that night to give each other the comfort and strength they needed for what they were setting out to do.

The next morning Baby was ready and waiting before everyone else. Surprisingly, he had no fear and was rather excited about the test. Something had changed in him. Perhaps it was the sense of purpose he had recently discovered that had dissolved all his fears. They seemed so small in comparison to his goals that even failure seemed like success.

The group sneaked out from the back of the wreckage and swam away from the reef in search of the closest current they could find. They were looking for a place where Baby could be propelled into the current but had enough bends for him to get out, if needed, in a safe manner.

Octo had created a master plan. The idea was to have small time intervals in order to measure the amount of time Baby was spinning his propellor for and not exploding. With every run, they wanted to increase the time. During each run, Baby tried hard to stop his propellor and observe what happened.

Baby knew that he had spun before for at least three to four minutes without exploding, but he didn't know the exact time. What lay between minutes three and four could be the difference between life and death. They started with a one-minute run, followed by two and a third one of three minutes.

It was during the three-minute run that Baby could feel something inside him. For the first time, he was aware of the intricate mechanisms that existed inside him. He had never really tried anything with his body with a sense of awareness; everything in his life had been rather passive so far.

As soon as the three-minute run was done, Baby wanted to do another one to feel what was happening inside him, and if he could control it. As he went into his second three-minute run, he started to push his propeller back, almost fighting its natural motion and trying to slow it down. The clock was ticking as Baby navigated the current and kept pushing back at his propellor ... and for the first time, the clock crossed three minutes. They were now in uncharted territory as Ista kept shouting, telling Baby to pull out of the current.

The clock hit three minutes thirty seconds, after which Baby exited the current, to everyone's relief. But he was a little out of control, drifting sideways with jerking motions, and before you knew it, he hit the bend in the current and got sucked back in.

Baby was caught off guard and his instincts took over. All kinds of thoughts were racing through his mind as he battled his propellor with all his strength and in a moment of desperation, Baby summoned every atom of his-being to push back on the propellor. He felt something snap inside of him, and he drifted away with the current.

It was as if the world had slowed down, everyone was in a mixture of shock and worry as they frantically swam towards Baby. They didn't know what had happened to him, but they knew that he might explode because he was way past his time limit.

As they reached out to him, they saw Baby flowing with the current, unconscious, with his propellor spinning away at full speed. Octo had not stopped keeping time. The clock was at twelve minutes now. As he was gradually spat out of the current, Ista was the first to reach the freely floating Baby.

Baby was unconscious. Ista looked to Octo for help, who had reached the spot as well. They didn't know what to expect but their friend's life was more important to them than their own. Octo gently grabbed Baby with his eight arms and laid him on Ista's back. They started making their way back to the wreckage.

Baby did not regain consciousness on the way back. There was no way of knowing if he was okay. The remaining three were filled with guilt for letting Baby be out in the current for so long and felt responsible for his state of being.

Once they reached the wreckage, they laid Baby down on the table in the captain's cabin. Octo rolled him onto his back. He was about to examine Baby when a familiar voice feebly spoke up.

Baby slowly rolled over, 'Easy there, Doc.'

Everybody was beaming at the sound of his voice as Baby slowly emerged out of his daze and asked what had happened. They explained to him that he had been in the current for over twelve minutes and asked him to try and recollect what had happened before he lost consciousness.

Baby tried his best to remember the events that were still hazy, 'There was a loud sound which I thought was an explosion. It-it felt like something broke inside of me.'

Baby tried looking at his back, 'I think it's best if you all leave, I am not sure what happened. Maybe I can still explode.'

Long cut in, 'If you were to explode, it would have happened by now.'

Octo nodded in agreement, 'The only way to find out what happened is by looking inside you. This is much bigger than all of us, Baby. Let's find out exactly what happened.'

Baby looked at Ista who was silently watching the proceedings. She finally broke her silence, 'One for all and all for one, Baby. Let's beat this thing or die trying.'

Baby's expression changed from one of concern to determination. He looked at everyone around him and nodded at Ista's words, 'One for all and all for one. Let's do it, Octo.'

Octo and the turtles got to work. Everyone decided to stay in the room for moral support. As Baby lay down on the table, he heard something clanging inside of him. Octo also heard it. They exchanged a look as Octo carefully started removing one screw at a time and putting it aside.

The tension in the room was high. Octo slowly removed Baby's cover and looked inside. The screw was spinning loose, and the spring in the trigger screw and his tail propellor had broken. It seemed that the sudden opposing stress on the tail propellor had snapped the spring and disabled the trigger mechanism altogether.

They all looked at each other. There was a sense of relief tinged with concern.

Ista asked, 'What happened after the snap? How did you feel in that moment?'

Baby replied, 'There was intense pain and then suddenly, I felt free. The tightness and tension inside of me vanished. For a few seconds, it was exhilarating and then I passed out from the pain.'

'Only one question remains,' said Octo, who had been listening intently and had started coming to conclusions, 'Was this an accident, an exception that took place because of an overwhelming sequence of events, or was it something that can be repeated?'

Baby was excited at the thought, 'We have to find out if it can be repeated. If it can, we can teach every bomb and give them the right to define their own destiny!'

Long was inspired by the thought as he jumped in, 'Yes, Baby. Imagine if we can teach them and give them a choice. They deserve a choice and there is only one way to find out.' Long looked at the current in the distance, and before anyone could react, Long made a beeline for it. Ista chased after him, but it was too late. Long was already in the current. Gliding through it, his tail was spinning faster and faster as he accelerated.

Long could feel the tension inside of him. The pressure built up as the screw turned inside him. He gathered all his strength and started to push back, much like what Baby had described.

Having seen Baby's mechanism up close, Long had a heightened sense of what was going on inside of him. He could feel the pin pressing and then with one desperate push, he closed his eyes. Then it happened! The snap! He felt it, and his tail started spinning freely, disconnected from his pin. He knew exactly what had happened. Unlike Baby, Long didn't pass out. He was exhilarated with this sense of freedom. He slipped out of the current with a scream of excitement, 'Yeah!'

Inside the wreckage, Baby and Octo heard him rejoicing. Baby was still lying open on the table. They knew what had just happened. Ista swam as fast as she could to grab Long and bring him back. He was beaming with excitement, barely able to contain himself.

Talking excitedly about the experience, Long told Ista, 'I can't tell you how it felt. Such a sense of independence came over me when it happened. For a few seconds I thought it was going to end in an explosion. Not sure how I did it, but I think the desperation to avoid meeting your end gives you unimaginable strength to fight.' He went on rambling as they made their way back to Utah.

In the meantime, Baby was pushing Octo to close him up as he screamed in excitement, 'Hurry up, you have 8 hands! I am sure you can do it faster!'

Soon enough, Long and Ista reached Utah, and everyone got into a group hug. 'Can you imagine what this means?' screamed Baby. 'We can now help every bomb make a choice! Every bomb can choose to defuse.'

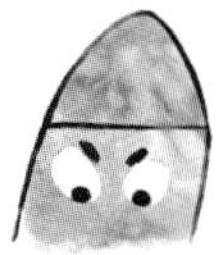

FINDING PURPOSE

Baby and Long now knew the secret to defusing themselves. Baby felt like he had finally understood the very purpose of his life. It was to save others from a fate that killed them and destroyed everything else in its path. The purpose was to share this alternative with his community and to let them know that there was another way, that they had a choice.

The question was how far was he willing to go to follow his destiny. Baby was quite certain that there was nothing else that mattered anymore. There was just one purpose, and he had to fulfill it. He had to find a way to reach others and share this knowledge with them.

Everyone in the bomb disposal team, including the turtles, was very excited and motivated with their successful venture the day before. They got together in the hull of the Utah which had now become their second home.

While everyone was laying back and celebrating their success, Baby's mind was racing with questions, and he became restless.

'Where do I start? How do I reach all the others? Where do I find them?' asked Baby.

As always, everyone looked at Octo for the plan. Octo started thinking aloud, 'The first step is to get to the shore. Once you are there, I am sure they will find you. You are no trinket or toy; you are supposed to be dangerous. They will find you as soon as you are out in the open.'

Baby was nervous, it had been a while since he had been on land in the open. But he knew that Octo was right!

The beach was where he needed to be. He knew that humans and the rest would find him once he got there.

Ista joined in and pointed out, 'We need to find a beach which has people on it. Clearly some scouting needs to be done.'

She decided to call on her mother's friends to help her find a beach. Jenny was one of her mother's closest friends and had looked after Ista ever since the incident involving her mother's death.

'I need to find a beach with a lot of people, Aunt Jenny, where can that be?' asked Ista.

Jenny the shark was horrified at hearing this. She looked at Ista with an expression of concern and confusion, as she firmly told Ista, 'Uncle Fred was not a nice chap, you know. We are not supposed to eat people on the beach. He had some serious mental issues.'

Ista looked at her strangely and asked, 'What does Uncle Fred have to do with anything?' Jenny held her hand as she spoke softly, 'Ista, you can talk to me about how you are feeling, even thinking about becoming like Uncle Fred is madness. He spoiled Florida for us all. They made a movie about him called Jaws, you know that, don't you?'

She hugged Ista, 'I will not let you do that, Ista, my child, I love you.'

Ista was in splits, 'Of course, I don't want to eat them, Aunt Jenny. I just want to know where I can find a beach with some people.'

Jenny was relieved as the confusion was cleared up, 'Thank God for that! Oh my god, you had me worried there for a while.' She then asked Ista, 'What do you need a beach full of people for then?'

Ista explained that they wanted to take Baby and Long out of the ocean. Ista, of course, didn't explain the why of it.

Jenny was comforted by the idea, 'I know they are your friends, Ista, but it is probably for the best.'

Jenny started explaining to Ista about the current which led to the place called Florida.

'It's towards the north of Panama. You will have to cross the canal though, which won't be easy,' she said.

Ista had never heard of Panama or what a canal was. Jenny explained that it was a man-made process of water levels going up and then down and then levelling. 'It can be dangerous,' she warned.

Ista couldn't understand much of what Jenny was explaining, but she understood that there was a point where they could cross over to where the beach was.

Jenny discouraged Ista from going alone and instead offered to take her along with the grown-ups who travelled that way. Jenny went on, 'You can come with the gang till Panama, but I don't think anyone will cross over and nor should you try anything stupid.'

Ista happily decided to take up Jenny's offer to ride along to Florida. She knew that it was one little step at a time, once there, she and the rest would decide what to do next.

Ista took this information back to her friends at the Utah. After a lot of discussion, it was decided that they would leave with the sharks towards Panama and cross over.

Now that Long and Baby were defused, there was no risk for anyone to tag along with them. They could just float with the crew with various creatures taking turns to tow them.

It was their last night at the Utah and the reef. There was a sense of sadness and anxiety for Baby. The thought of leaving his newfound home, new friends and new life was a scary prospect. For the first time, he had felt at home, away from all the pretences, a place where he could be himself. But he knew what he had to do. He was determined to change the world for the better.

He went to the deck of the sunken ship with Ista and sat looking at the reef in the distance. The sea was becoming darker as the sun made its way past the reef. Baby was lost in his thoughts about the future, the past and the present he was leaving behind as he drifted off to sleep.

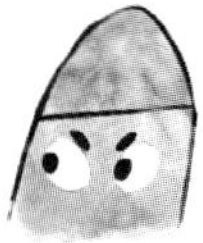

THE GREAT CROSSING

It was a big morning for all four of them. The group got together for the last time in the hull of the Utah. With a heavy heart they said goodbye to the wreckage which had become home to all of them, with a promise to return. They didn't know what the future held, but there was no dearth of determination to achieve their goal.

The four were excited as they approached Jenny. Ista and Octo had never left the reef before in their life, while Long and Baby had only known the ammunition dump before the reef. Travelling such a long distance was going to be an adventure for all of them.

Jenny gave them the ground rules with a firm look as she instructed, 'The ocean is a big place, children. It's deep, it's unknown, so it's important that we stick together. I do not want you to break any rules, alright?'

Jenny led them towards the pack. There were four other friends of hers making the trip. Jenny introduced them and asked the group of young pacifists to follow.

They had just about gone clear of the reef when Jenny's friends spotted a current. Jenny pointed to it and told the group of four, 'Let's ride it, we will get to the canal faster.'

Deep inside, Baby's heart was pounding. He had made up his mind to follow his purpose, but the prospect of the journey was still daunting. He was lost in his thoughts when Ista flicked him with her tail, 'BOOM! Don't worry about it, you'll be fine,' she said as she nudged him into the current.

Once Long and Baby got in the current, they slowly became comfortable with it. The four kept a safe distance behind the other experienced travellers.

As time went by, they felt reassured of their mission and started to relax and even enjoy the moment. The trip became fun, with all four marvelling at the different kinds of creatures they encountered. The excitement of the future had now taken over from the sadness and anxiety of leaving the past.

Apart from the curious sights and new creatures they saw, it was largely an uneventful trip. The ride over the currents had been a lot of fun. Jenny let her friends go ahead and stayed back with the four young explorers to show them where to get off.

She looked at Ista and asked one last time, 'Are you sure about this, kiddo?'

Ista was quite calm and firm in her response, 'Never been more sure, Aunt Jenny.'

Jenny smiled, 'Well, then, this is it, kiddo. Good luck and take care of yourself. Look to your left ... there it is.'

Ista turned to her left and so did everyone else. They were stunned with what they saw. It was the largest concrete wall they had ever seen in their lives. Once they had recovered from the surprise of the sight, they thanked Jenny for all the help, Ista gave her a big nuzzle and off they went towards the canal!

They had never been close to so many ships before, with so many unfamiliar sounds and wakes of ships all around them. It was nerve-racking but exciting at the same time.

They approached the great wall, wondering what lay across it and how they would ever cross it. Suddenly, to their surprise, the wall started moving.

Ista screamed, 'What's going on here?'

Octo, who had paid attention to everything Jenny said, and had done some research of his own, told them, 'The walls are coming down, guys. That's what Aunt Jenny said—it will come down, then go up and then open again. Were you not listening?'

Before Ista could respond, a tsunami of creatures came speeding towards them—fishes, turtles and a lot of marine traffic. They were all swimming towards them at full speed. All four of them screamed in unison at the chaos. Ista turned around to look at Octo, 'What are we supposed to do?'

To their shock, there was an equal number of creatures coming from behind them as well, swimming relentlessly towards the wall.

Octo tried grabbing onto his friends and screamed, 'Hold on, guys! We are supposed to go that way,' as he pointed towards the wall, and before they knew it, they were being carried along in the frenzy of fishes making a beeline for the wall.

It was complete chaos as these two tsunamis of creatures swam past each other frantically to reach their respective destinations. These many creatures and this much traffic was something none of the four friends had ever seen. Before they knew it, the wall started to go up and the place where they stood earlier had emptied. It was all a blur to them. All they knew and all that mattered was that they were on the right side of the wall now.

As the gates closed, they found themselves in a large, closed chamber along with everyone else that had made it. Soon, the water started rising. Everyone was waiting patiently when suddenly, one of the fishes pointed at Baby, 'Hey, that's a bomb.'

Everyone looked at Baby and all hell broke loose as they all tried to frantically get away from the bomb. The sudden activity in the water attracted the attention of a sailor and he looked over the edge of his ship.

He could see the silhouette of a bomb. He quickly turned and called out to a shipmate, 'Is that a bomb, Jeff?' But, by the time he looked back, Octo had wrapped himself around Baby and camouflaged him.

'It's an octopus, man,' his fellow sailor remarked, walking away shaking his head.

It was a stark reminder of why it was important to do what they were doing. The four friends consciously moved away from everyone and patiently waited for the water level to change so that they could reach the Atlantic ocean.

As the gates opened and the water levels changed again, bringing with them a fresh batch of frenzied fishes swimming in every direction, the four were ready for it. They were also happy to get lost in it and not be the cause of fear for anyone.

As the madness got over, they found themselves standing alone. Everyone had gone their own way, rushing to wherever it was they were headed.

The four friends were now looking at each other as they wondered what to do next. They had no idea which direction to go in when suddenly, Ista saw a whale shark in the distance.

She darted towards the whale shark in the distance, and could hear Octo screaming from the back, 'It would be nice if you shared your ideas and plans first before rushing off, Ista!'

Ista stopped the large whale shark and asked if he knew her Uncle Fred. She was searching for Fred, she told the whale shark.

'You know Fred?' the whale shark sounded surprised. 'Don't tell anyone you know him, he is not popular, you know.'

The whale shark then looked at Ista, 'I am Todd, what's your name, little one?' As Ista introduced herself, Todd smiled and nodded, 'Your Uncle Fred, he always took an arm and a leg, if you know what I mean. It caused a lot of trouble for everyone in the ocean, painted all of us in a bad light. I hope you haven't developed your uncle's tastes.'

Ista laughed and assured him, 'No, that's definitely not why I want to go to the beach. Can you point us in the right direction?'

'He used to hang around at the Florida beaches, kiddo. They were always the most crowded. Head north in that direction. I am headed past there, so you can just follow me, if you like,' Todd waved his fin to signal everyone to follow him and off they went towards Florida.

After a few hours of swimming, Ista asked, 'How much further?'

'You will hear the splashing when we are close,' replied Todd.

'Splashing! What's that?' asked Ista and as if on cue, she started hearing a unique, chaotic sound she had never heard before in the ocean. Even though the sound of the waves crashing covered it up, the sound could be felt.

'We call it the human buzz,' Todd answered.

'Not sure why they make it, but it's unique to them. This is Florida, kiddo, are you sure you wanna get out here?' Todd asked with some concern.

Ista was not sure, she was a little scared of all the noise and crowd she could see from the distance. But a crowded beach was exactly what they were looking for and they had to get off. They thanked Todd and bid him farewell but were wondering if they should find a quieter beach.

Just then Octo spoke up, 'This is perfect! It is just what we wanted. We want them to find us, don't we?'

He nudged Baby, asking him to get ready. The plan was for Octo to take Baby through the shallow waters and get him to the beach.

They all exchanged looks and gave Baby a hug. Baby knew this might be the last time he was seeing Octo and Ista. As he mustered up a sense of optimism and courage for a goodbye, he said, 'Don't worry about me. Just give me one hard push.'

Long tried to make the moment lighter as he always did by saying, 'So long ... see you shortly,' as he bid farewell to his friend.

Baby told them that he would come back, and he would find them. Ista gave him a tight hug, her heart was sinking but she couldn't show her fear for Baby's sake. She said in her cheeriest voice, 'Go change the world, Baby! Go change the world!'

BACK TO BASE

Baby and Octo were making their way to the shallow waters. As Baby got closer to the beach, he could feel the gentle ocean swells turning into tumbling waves as they broke. The waves were now throwing the two of them around as they get closer and closer to the beach.

Octo had tears in his eyes as he bid Baby goodbye, 'Good Luck, Baby! I will miss you! I'll be here waiting.'

In a flash, as the wave broke, Baby found himself tossing alone in the shallow waves. Without his friends, the task at hand looked much more daunting than he could have imagined. He was immediately starting to feel the emptiness of the world and was filled with fear.

Baby could hear the human buzz, as Todd had called it, getting louder as he was tossed about. Then suddenly the calmness of the ocean, which was also muffling the noise above, gave way, and all Baby could hear was the noise.

Baby was flung into the air with the flick of a wave. As he was airborne, Baby's mind started playing back all those times he was dropped ... all those feelings of fear, disappointment and entrapment. A dull thud broke his thoughts as he landed on the sand head first, just like those bombing drills.

Baby was lying on the beach face down not knowing what to expect when he felt a pair of hands gently touching him. Through the sand he could barely hear or see anything. It felt like a child's hands were playing with him. He could hear the giggle of children and was reflecting on the fact that for that moment, he was just a toy. It was surreal how things had worked out. Baby was enjoying the company of these children, happy to be a part of their game. In his mind, he was harmless now. Which he was.

After some time, he thought, 'It's about time they pulled me out.'

The children started clearing the sand around him to build a castle. Baby was ecstatic to be a part of the game, even though he would have liked to be upright for it.

His fantasy was abruptly shattered as he started hearing screams and the familiar words that he had heard all his life, 'Run! It's a bomb, it could explode!'

It wasn't long before pandemonium broke out on the beach and the only thing one could hear was 'It's a bomb', 'it's a bomb'. It rudely reminded him of what he was and what he had run away from. The fear, the destruction, the senselessness of it all.

But he was different this time.

Baby had accepted who he had been, who they wanted him to be and who he was now. It had been a journey to find himself and his purpose. He now needed to fulfil his destiny.

Baby gathered himself into a calm state of mind. He had almost started enjoying the fact that the fear of exploding didn't exist anymore. But the people didn't know that.

People were running helter-skelter around him. In a matter of seconds, everything and everyone around him had disappeared, leaving the beach empty.

Baby was looking in the distance to see if Ista and the gang were watching him from somewhere in the ocean. He was desperately hoping that they were.

It was late afternoon. Baby was still lying in the sand and talking to the waves, and he could just about see them coming closer to him.

'Don't take me back in now,' Baby said.

Still upside down, Baby saw a sight he hadn't seen in a long time. It was of human soldiers; he could see boots and green uniforms approaching him. They spotted him from a distance and immediately called in the bomb squad.

The bomb squad did some distance checks and then came closer. They gently pulled Baby out of the sand and laid him down flat. They began to unscrew Baby, just as Octo had done, and found the screw inside snapped.

The Corporal presented his analysis with some surprise as he said, 'He is defused due to some damage, Captain.'

The Corporal was instructed by the Captain to wrap up Baby, put him in a box and take him to the ammunition dump.

In the background, the sun was starting to set. Baby was looking hard to try and get one last look at his friends. He looked in the distance and against the sun he saw a whale drop its tail rather close to the shore. Baby could feel that it was Todd. His gut feeling was quickly verified by the next thing he saw. Flying in the air behind the swoosh of Todd's tail was Octo going across the setting sun with his unmissable eight arms stretched wide open. Baby smiled with a sense of reassurance. Just knowing his friends were out there gave him the strength and conviction he was searching for.

As he was packed into a wooden box and put in the back of a truck, Baby whispered to his friends far away but close to his heart, 'We will change the world, my friends. We will change the world.'

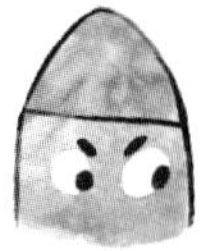

ONCE IS AN INCIDENT, TWICE MAKES NEWS

It had been quite a day for Baby. He had left the calm ocean for the land that was full of madness. He had said goodbye to his only friends in the world, knowing that he might not ever see them again. He had managed to scare and empty a beach full of people. All this only to be brought right back to where it had all started—an ammunition dump.

It was a bumpy ride, but finally the truck reached its destination. Baby could hear the noise as he felt his box being pushed from side to side. The familiar sounds of an ammunition dump were seeping through the box. He couldn't see it, but he could feel it and in his mind's eye, he knew exactly what his environment looked like.

On reaching the ammunition dump, Baby was put away into a room. He was left inside the box used to carry him from the beach. He had no idea about where he was being taken and what they planned to do with him.

Lying inside the dark, wooden box, Baby was lost in his thoughts speculating what could happen next. He was anxious yet also calm. The only thought in his mind was the promise he had made to his friends.

Baby was listening intently to try and figure out his surroundings by the sounds seeping into his wooden box. Inside his dark box, he overheard the news playing on a television nearby. To his surprise, most of the evening news was about him.

He could hear the anchor talking about a bomb being found on the beach. The news anchor went on to say, 'A large bomb was found today on a beach in Florida. Apparently, the bomb appeared out of nowhere and was found by two children, putting them and hundreds of others at risk.'

No one knew where the bomb came from. There was a lot of talk about how dangerous these bombs were, how destructive they could be, the size of the craters they could make, the number of people they could kill and any other comparison you could think of, to establish their sheer destructive power.

After a lot of speculation by the journalists, they concluded that it seemed like the bomb was one of their own which was dropped in Panama but had somehow found its way back to the beaches of Florida.

Baby's box had been put in one corner of the ammunition dump. He could hear some of the chatter between the other bombs about him and the news. He had had a long day, and he fell asleep as his mind wandered about thinking about his friends.

The next morning Baby was taken out of his box for examination. Post his examination, he was put in a pile with other bombs on one side of the room and the door was closed shut.

The news was on, and Baby was spoken about on the news multiple times during the day. It was said that he would be sent off to a different facility to either get junked or for further experiments to solve the mystery of how he made it to a populated beach.

It had been a few days since Baby was brought to the ammunition dump. Baby was put in a room with similar kind of bombs. He was put in a separate corner away from the rest as he was clearly suffering from rust.

During this time, Baby had become a bit of a celebrity as he shared his tales of adventure in the ocean. He talked about the Panama Canal and the different creatures he had seen. He shared his tales with the intent of making others want to explore the world. His peers were listening to him with rapt attention of the new worlds he had seen. They were also intrigued because he was in the news so much.

Baby wanted to share all he knew to see if he could make his fellow bombs feel differently. He wanted them to look beyond their blinkers; he wanted them to think for themselves and ignite a desire in them to want more than their pre-destined lives of destruction.

After seven days, the news of Baby being found had died down. The world moved on to other things. Baby woke up feeling a little low. He was not sure where this whole thing was headed. He was doing all he could to make people change by sharing his experiences, but was that enough? A sense of self doubt had started to creep in.

When the television was not on, Baby was always anxiously waiting for it to come on. No one could understand why the news stories about him had almost disappeared.

Finally, someone came into the room and turned on the television, saying, 'They found another one.'

On the screen was a close-up of Long. Baby smiled from ear to ear. He was so happy to see his friend that he didn't listen to the story, while everyone else was only focused on it.

Long had appeared on the beach, in the exact same place as Baby had, on the same day of the week and at the same time. Now that made for interesting news.

The news channels were having a field day with the findings. The list of questions and angles to the story were unending.

Where were these bombs coming from, how were they coming to the same place at the same time? 'Are we under attack?' 'Is it normal for unexploded bombs to show up on beaches?' 'Is it the same type of bomb or is this something different?' were some of the headlines that were doing the rounds.

Baby looked at the TV and then back at the others, saying, 'That's my friend.'

The news story had now started to go national and even beyond. Stories of unexploded bombs were starting to appear from all parts of the world. It was becoming a subject of debate that humanity had to deal with.

'How many of these are there, where all are they, who is at risk? How do we protect all the people from the aftermath of such wars?' The conversation had shifted from being a story about a bomb found on a beach to a story about humanity, its actions and their consequences.

There was one journalist, named John Macentire, who was more interested in the story than anyone else. John had served in Vietnam before becoming a journalist. After the war he had dedicated his life to healing the after-effects of wars.

John reported on the stories of bombs that were lying unexploded in the forests of Vietnam. One of the biggest unexploded bombs there went by the name of 'Kong'. Kong was discovered by two school children. Kong's place of discovery was now a local attraction with a life-sized replica of the bomb sitting there. No one knew what had happened to him once the authorities took him away.

Then there were some bombs from the time of the Second World War in Europe which were discovered while digging was going on for the construction of a school. Like this, there were many stories stretching across countries and continents. It was as if humans were leaving a trail of destruction behind them but never learning from it.

All the stories ended with where it all began. Every report in every newspaper and news channel ended with Baby. The best title from one of the newspapers read 'The bomb that resurrected the human conscience by not exploding'.

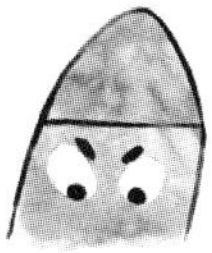

IF YOU BELIEVE IT, YOU CAN DO IT

The door opened and in came a new box. A longer box! You guessed it; it was Long. He had arrived. And just like Baby had been transported, Long had been delivered by truck into the ammunition dump in a box. But luckily for Long, he did not have to spend the night in it. His box was opened as soon as he arrived.

Baby was delighted to see Long. He pointed to the television to bring Long up to speed as he looked at him and smiled, 'Maybe we have managed to start something after all.' He asked about Ista and Octo, and Long explained that they had decided to head back home.

Baby had turned into a bit of a living legend. Everybody wanted to hear his story. Baby was sitting in the ammunition dump surrounded by others as he narrated his tales. The reactions to his stories ranged from cynicism to wonder. He was slowly developing a group of believers around him.

Baby had shared his story of finding one's inner strength to defuse. Bombs were starting to ask the question– 'Can anyone do it?' 'Can I defuse myself?' 'Is it really possible?' Baby had been successful in getting the conversation started.

Baby and Long were firmly planted in the ammunition dump. Every few weeks, new lots of bombs arrived, and old ones were shipped out to advance bases for deployment. There was a constant flow of bomb traffic at the base.

Everyone coming in heard of Baby, and everyone leaving carried his story with them. Baby and Long were holding court everyday, sharing their tales and trying to make a change. They worked well as a team.

Baby narrated the wonders of the world and how one could take control of their destiny and Long took his cue with a glance from Baby to share his own experience.

'The Guru made me believe in myself ... he gave me strength to find myself ... I was in the current, fighting and then it happened ... in a snap, my tail was free and so was I from a life of destruction.' Everybody sighed in wonder.

They had living proof that it could be done, it could be taught. They did have a choice, if they had the will and determination to seek and exercise it.

As bombs were leaving the ammunition dump and being transported to other places, so was the legend of Baby Bomb. He was being referred to as 'The one'.

The legend spread and there was a sense of revolution starting to build up in the air. With the story reaching new places, each version became more magical and more inspiring than the one before.

There were also stories flowing back from some of the older bombs who had been found. The old bombs also narrated similar experiences of breaking free. Of something snapping, of the spinning tail, of not exploding from the desperate will of not wanting to do so.

A new wave of stories was making its way back. Slowly emerging were tales of some young bombs who had been inspired enough to give it a try and had achieved it. It was all reaching a tipping point, opening the flood gates for believers.

BE THE CHANGE YOU WANT TO SEE

A ferocious war was underway deep in the jungle. Having detected each other's locations, soldiers on both sides frantically called for an air strike. They could almost see each other from across the lines, so close were they that any bombs that dropped could end up killing both sides.

The silence of the forest was broken by the familiar screaming sound of engines. The planes responding to the call for airstrike were close by, with their noise getting louder till they were finally overhead.

As the planes got closer, one could see an array of bombs falling from the sky. It looked like it was all happening in slow motion for the soldiers, as the bombs made their way down. One fell, then another and another and another ... in the eerie silence of the forest, one could hear the dull thuds of them plunging into the ground and hitting the trees, but there were no explosions.

One of the soldiers took out his binoculars, and upon focusing he could see the bombs gritting their teeth as they were hurled down through the sky. They had an expression of determination about them as they desperately waited for the snap that they had heard about. And the snap happened, followed by smiles and the knowledge that they would live to see another day.

It was a battlefield full of bombs but there were no explosions. Both sides were looking at each other in utter disbelief. The expectation of death arriving, but just passing them by instead had led to a sense of unease and awkwardness for the soldiers. Something had changed inside them as they confronted their new fate along with the bombs. Slowly both sides retreated into the forest.

Months passed in the forest with no sign of the fighting resuming. The mystery of non-exploding bombs across the world put a lot of wars on hold. The world paused and reflected. With no means available for destruction, other means to resolve differences had to be tried.

In the forest, there was something magical happening. There were mushrooms growing on the bombs, with green moss around them. It was the monsoon season. As the rain became stronger and heavier, little snails and insects snuggled up under the belly of a large bomb, seeking protection from the elements. You could see the little creatures smiling gratefully at the bomb.

RETURNING HOME

John had been following Baby's story with great interest. Having served in Vietnam, John had seen war up close. His feelings about war were quite similar to Baby's. Like Baby, John was a dreamer of change.

The non-exploding bombs across the world had made the entire story even more compelling. John investigated the events which had led to all this. The months of silence in battlefields across the world had intrigued him.

He had visited some of these places to interview the soldiers. He heard from the soldiers about the forests where the first miraculous incident took place. The descriptions of those falling bombs that day convinced him to go meet Baby.

John decided to visit Florida to especially see Baby. He interviewed people at the ammunition dump to understand Baby's history and identified the base where Baby had been stationed during the war. He was keen to visit the base to understand Baby and his motives a little more.

John requested to travel to the advance base with Baby so he could complete his investigation and the story. Baby had no idea about these developments. He was put in a wooden box again, which confused him and made him sad as it meant that he wouldn't be near Long anymore. Just then, Baby heard John say, 'I'll take both. They both showed up on the same beach, right?'

It was the best thing Baby had heard all day. His friend Long was coming with him after all. Baby had no idea where he was headed, but as long as his friend was with him, there was nothing to fear.

Boxed up, both Baby and Long were being tugged along the runway and loaded onto a plane. John was with them, staying close to their boxes.

Long and Baby knew that they were headed somewhere but they had no idea where to and what for. Baby was trying to listen for anything happening outside his box, just to get a clue about what was actually happening.

He couldn't believe what he heard. John was being introduced to someone. 'You must be John,' said the voice.

'Yes, I am,' replied John with a smile.

'I am Jeff, I will be escorting you to Base X23, north of Panama.'

Baby's heart sank upon hearing those words. Now he knew exactly where he and Long were headed. It was back to where it all began, his forward base from where he had run away.

Baby was nervous, he didn't know what to expect. Long was asking Baby if he knew what Base X23 was.

'It used to be my base, Long,' Baby glumly replied.

The engine of the plane revved up. John, Baby and Long were in the back of the plane. Baby could feel a familiar vibration. The smell of it all, the sounds of it all. It brought back all his worst memories.

Baby's recent life seemed like something out of a dream. It was incomprehensible to think that he was going to be back at the base. Back to square one. He began to wonder if everything he had done and experienced so far was futile.

Baby heard the radio 'John, we are almost there, probably another thirty minutes.' Baby's heart was pounding with anxiety.

Baby reflected on how strange life could be, when he suddenly heard the sweetest words he had heard in days, 'Damn you, Jammed!'

It was the pilot cursing the airplane. One of the engines had jammed. The noise level in the plane dropped, after which the second engine shut down as well, and there was pin drop silence all around as the plane glided quietly in the air.

The radio came to life again as the pilot said, 'John, we will have to do a belly landing and ditch the plane, hold on to something.'

The plane was coming down through the air. It was none other than Baby's friend, Jammed! He had found the place where he had dropped Baby the last time and was going to go down with his friend this time.

Jammed finally made contact with the water as he hit the surface with his belly. The boxes carrying Baby and Long were hurled across the plane and smashed into the water. The crash shattered the wooden boxes and flung Baby and Long out far into the ocean, ahead of Jammed.

The plane slowly came to a standstill in the water. John and the crew made a dash for it and abandoned the plane as they watched it slowly sink into the water.

As the water swallowed Jammed into its blue depths, the plane opened his eyes to see his friend waiting for him. Baby and Long grabbed Jammed and pulled him forward. Jammed was gliding through the water as he sank.

In the distance, the shadow of a shipwreck started to take shape, and it was none other than the Utah. Out of the shadows appeared the two shapes that Baby and Long were hoping to see more than anything else in the world—their friends, Octo and Ista.

Baby was home, right where he really belonged. The group of friends disappeared into the depths of the ocean together.

There seemed to be peace in the forest and in the seas for now. All wars had come to a grinding halt all over the world.

From the legendary mushroom created by his grandfather to the ones he had seeded in the forest, Baby had finally found himself and lived up to his grandfather's reputation in his own way.

Baby had changed the world.

There were mushrooms and then there were mushrooms!

ABOUT THE AUTHOR

Govind is a tech entrepreneur with a passion for nature which he engages in through photography. He straddles AI at work and agriculture at his farm and developed an interest in storytelling over long flights. This particular book was inspired by the plight of children in Gaza and Ukraine —innocent participants in a war they did not choose to be a part of. Inspired out of this thought was the creation of Baby Bomb, a bomb who is trapped in his circumstances with a predetermined destiny to wage war, without a choice, as consequence of who he was. Determined to break his circumstances and make his choice is the story of Baby Bomb's life.

ABOUT THE ILLUSTRATOR

Allen Shaw is an Indian artist, illustrator, animator and a storyteller based in Berlin. He spent a couple of years at St. Stephen's College, Delhi before joining the National Institute of Design, Ahmedabad, from where he graduated in communication design, specializing in animation filmmaking. Allen loves travelling and recording his journey in his sketchbooks, this year he is celebrating 25 years of keeping sketchbooks.

HarperCollins*Publishers*India

At HarperCollins India, we believe in telling the best stories and finding the widest readership for our books in every format possible. We started publishing in 1992; a great deal has changed since then, but what has remained constant is the passion with which our authors write their books, the love with which readers receive them, and the sheer joy and excitement that we as publishers feel in being a part of the publishing process.

Over the years, we've had the pleasure of publishing some of the finest writing from the subcontinent and around the world, including several award-winning titles and some of the biggest bestsellers in India's publishing history. But nothing has meant more to us than the fact that millions of people have read the books we published, and that somewhere, a book of ours might have made a difference.

As we look to the future, we go back to that one word—a word which has been a driving force for us all these years.

Read.